Daisy Rothschild

Betty Leslie-Melville

Daisy
Rothschild

Doubleday & Company, Inc., Garden City, New York

To
my joy—my grandson
Garrick,
who lives in Africa
and
helps take care of Daisy.

The publisher and the author wish to thank the following
for photographs appearing in this book: Marion Gordon, pp. 3, 9,
18, 29, 33, 37; Esmond Bradley Martin, p. 4; and Franke Keating, p. 40.
All other photographs are from the author's collection.

Designed by Virginia M. Soulé

Library of Congress Cataloging-in-Publication Data

Leslie-Melville, Betty.
   Daisy Rothschild.

   Includes index.
   Summary: The author describes her relationship with a
Rothschild giraffe, a nearly extinct species, in Kenya.
   1. Daisy Rothschild (Giraffe)—Juvenile literature.
2. Giraffe —Biography—Juvenile literature. 3. Rare
animals—Juvenile literature. [1. Daisy Rothschild
(Giraffe) 2. Giraffe. 3. Rare animals] I. Title.
QL795.G55L46 1987   599.73′57   86-29070
ISBN 0-385-23895-9
ISBN 0-385-23896-7 (lib. bdg.)

Introduction

Kenya is a country filled with animals. It is on the east coast of Africa. Nairobi is its big city, just seventy-six miles south of the equator.

Many of the animals are being killed, and among certain kinds there are so few left, they are called endangered species. We try to keep them from being poached (killed for their meat and skin). One particular endangered species we have saved is the Rothschild giraffe.

What is a Rothschild giraffe? It is the largest of the three different species of giraffe in Kenya, it is the only one that has pure white legs, and the male (bull) has two extra horns behind its two main ones. (In addition to the two main horns, all giraffe also have a small one on their forehead.) The Rothschild giraffe used to be called only the "five-horned giraffe" until Walter Rothschild, a botanist, noticed the difference and registered them in his name.

Giraffe are the only animals born with horns. They are six feet tall when born and for the first year grow about one inch a week. They grow to be eighteen feet tall, yet they have only seven vertebrae in their long necks—the same as people and mice. Giraffe live to be thirty-five years old.

Many people think they don't make a sound, but we have heard ours make a loud, deep grunt many times.

My husband and I are the only people in the world who have successfully raised wild baby giraffe.

This is how it happened.

Chapter 1

I met my husband, Jock, in Kenya. We were married there and bought a big, old stone house, on the outskirts of Nairobi, that we loved. We loved looking at Mount Kilimanjaro, 110 miles away, and walking in the forest. But best of all was the surprise we got when we saw three wild Maasi giraffe on our property and realized they lived there, too. It was a thrilling sight to see the tallest animals in the world standing in front of the tallest mountain in Africa. We would sit in our living room and watch them strolling down the driveway, munching the trees they fancied, destroying our shrubs, and stomping the flowers along the way. We named them Tom, Dick, and Harry.

One day a friend came to see us and said he had the only 130 Rothschild giraffe left in the world living on his ranch, and that they were being poached. He asked us, "Would you take just one? You'd be helping to save an endangered species. At least there would be one Rothschild *twiga* [Swahili for "giraffe"] left."

"If we got a baby giraffe," I said enthusiastically to Jock, "it would live outside and just eat the trees, and we wouldn't have to do anything. . . ." Ha, little did I know.

"But how do we get one?" Jock asked.

"Baby giraffe and sea lions are the two animals that can't take tranquilizers," our friend told us, "but I know a man who knows how to capture a baby giraffe from his horse. His name is Rutherfurd, and his horse's name is Douglas."

So Rutherfurd came to see us and promised to try to rope a baby giraffe for us. "Then we'll put it in a stable up there and give it a little milk for a few days. After that, we'll bring it to Nairobi." He didn't mention how dangerous the capture might be. Nor did he tell us that if he was successful at getting one, we would have to give it a bottle of milk four times a day for a year.

So, the following week, we merrily drove the 225 miles north to the ranch for the big event.

Early the next morning, Rutherfurd introduced us to Douglas, the only horse in the world able to attempt this hazardous undertaking. By nature, horses are terrified of giraffe. It had taken Rutherfurd three years to train Douglas to go into a herd. As if that were not bad enough, the land where the Rothschild giraffe live is dangerous because it is pocked with ant-bear holes two feet wide and three feet deep, hidden in the long grass. The nocturnal ant bears, or aardvarks, dig these enormous holes in a matter of minutes while searching for termites, and whether they find their food or not, the holes remain for years afterward, camouflaged by grass. It is impossible to drive a vehicle over the land, and no one in his right mind would ride a horse over it—no one but Rutherfurd, that is. And no one but Rutherfurd would ride Douglas, who is also said to be crazy.

Watching a large herd through his binoculars, Rutherfurd found a giraffe to try for. He kicked Douglas, and they were off like kamikaze pilots. Douglas concentrated on the ground, not having any idea where he was going, and Rutherfurd concentrated on the herd like a guided missile beamed into its target aircraft. To protect their babies, giraffe get them out front, as far away from the danger as possible, so Rutherfurd had to bore through the entire herd. The giraffe were running at a fantastic rate, flying hooves striking out at him, just missing him over and over again. He looked like a scurrying ant alongside the speeding giants. He looked as if he were drowning in giraffe. Some of the giraffe stumbled into ant-bear holes, turned somersaults, and rolled back on their feet again.

The large herd ran in fear.

There was so much dust and confusion that for a moment we couldn't see Rutherfurd. But suddenly we saw him emerge in front of the herd, galloping after a baby. Riveted, watching through binoculars, we then saw him, still at full gallop, come alongside the little giraffe, reach out and throw his arm around its neck, then leap off Douglas and wrestle the baby to the ground. If Rutherfurd won the match, we'd have a giraffe; if the giraffe won, we'd have a funeral.

We picked our way through low bushes and grass so high we were unable to see, but soon we could just see Rutherfurd's head—and something else.

Rutherfurd called, "It's a girl!"

Douglas and Rutherfurd come alongside the little giraffe.

And there she lay in the short marshy grass, her feet tied by a rope, with Rutherfurd struggling to hold her neck upright. (A giraffe's head must be kept up because if the animal lies prone or its head goes down, it can die in a matter of minutes from undigested food blocking its windpipe.)

We had picked out names in advance, so we went up and introduced ourselves to Daisy Rothschild, telling her we were her new parents. For us it was love at first sight, but she hated us. Her enormous eyes glared at us in fright, and those long, long eyelashes made her look like a very angry Daisy indeed. We touched her—she was so soft and silky. I kissed her nose, I patted her head, I stroked her mane, which was a golden brown. Her little horns were tufted—they looked like two black paint-brushes sticking up out of her head. Three spots shaped just like butterflies ran down her beige neck in a row. She was so beautiful.

Rutherfurd slipped a rope over her head, untied her feet, and let her stand. That was when the fight began. I spoke to her softly and told her we loved her; she kicked us. Her front legs flew out at us at a terrible speed with a forward and downward punch, her neck was arched— she looked like a sea horse. We walked her, fighting all the way, to our minibus. Have you ever tried to get an angry giraffe into a minibus? Somehow we finally managed to shove her in and drove through the pocked land to the stable.

Chapter 2

We dragged Daisy, still kicking wildly, out of the bus and into the stable, which we had padded with straw. After trying unsuccessfully to escape, she just stood there staring at us, obviously disturbed. Rutherfurd said we should leave her alone for a few hours while she got used to her surroundings. That evening we peeped in and found her just standing there motionless and looking miserable.

The next morning, we raced to the stables to find her standing in the same place. Rutherfurd said she would have to drink by the following morning or she would die of dehydration. All day, we sat taking turns holding out the pan of milk and talking to her. Of course, she had never seen a pan before and had no idea what it was. She wanted nothing to do with it and would not drink. As the day wore on, she looked even more unhappy.

We were so worried.

At dawn, we raced to her to find her so weak she was unable to stand. I started to cry, and Daisy actually had a tear in her eye, too. I could imagine her asking,

Daisy actually had a tear in her eye.

"Why can't I run in the sunshine and sleep near my mother and drink her good milk? Where is she? Who are all these strange creatures who do not look like giraffe at all?" Yet I knew if we hadn't captured her, she would be dead within a year.

Forty-nine hours passed, and I feared she was going to die right then. But suddenly, for no apparent reason, she got to her feet, walked to the bowl of milk that Jock was holding, and put her face into it and drank! And drank! She seemed so surprised it was milk. She licked her mouth and nose, then looked at Jock, bent down, and kissed him—and from that minute on, Jock was her "mother"! Then she investigated our hands and put her head close to ours and sniffed us. We spoke softly to her all the time, but didn't try to touch her. A few hours later, we gave her some more milk. She sucked at it and sort of inhaled it, like some berserk vacuum cleaner. It would be all over her face and up her nostrils, but she'd just stick out her long, purple tongue and poke it up her nose. Then she'd drink some more, and, spluttering, she'd spray us thoroughly. Since the milk had lots of cod liver oil in it, in no time Jock and I smelled terrible.

The next morning, when we walked toward her stable, she had her leg out the top half of the door trying to get to her "mother," Jock, for more milk. Afterward she let us stroke her face and ears. She felt as soft as velvet.

Jock became Daisy's "mother," which saved her life.

We picked her some thorn tree branches that had yellow flowers blooming on them. She recognized them as her favorite food and seemed delighted as she nibbled away.

Watching your baby giraffe eating yellow flowers is like watching a real live birthday card.

Veterinarians and scientists had warned us of the difficulties we would have raising a giraffe. Although other people in Kenya had tried, none had been successful. A doctor of zoology, who had raised many wild animals, but not giraffe, told us the most important thing is love. He told us about a baby steenbok, a species of antelope extremely difficult to rear, that he had seen in a mechanic's garage hopping about the spare parts and rusty wrecks of cars. The African had found the little thing abandoned and fed it and took it with him everywhere. Asked what he fed it, the mechanic told him whatever he had to eat himself—sometimes a doughnut, a sandwich, sometimes some soup served in an old hubcap. It was then that the doctor, who had tried and tried unsuccessfully to raise a steenbok with vitamins and calcium and sophisticated drugs, suddenly realized that wild animals need love as much as food if they are to survive. He was adamant as he told us, "They must relate to one person, they must be loved by that person. Then they will imprint and live." (Imprinting is when an animal feels attached, or bonded, to another.)

Already Jock was Daisy's "mother," so we had hope.

Daisy loves thorn tree flowers.

The next morning, with the help of about six other men, we got Daisy sitting in the minibus for her journey to Nairobi.

At one point, Jock drove into a gas station. You can imagine the surprise on the attendant's face when he saw a giraffe in the minibus. He didn't have enough money to go to game parks, so he had never seen a giraffe before, and he thanked us for bringing her.

Daisy's head poked out the top of the minibus even though she was sitting down.

We finally pulled into our own driveway and parked near Daisy's boma (pen), which we had built for her. We slid her out and untied her fetters. Slowly and stiffly she stood up, and we gave her a gentle shove into her home.

Immediately she accepted some warm milk from Jock. It was cold in Nairobi, so in the back of our car we found a tarpaulin that was torn and ragged and smelled of oil and gas and peanut butter. We hung it in a corner of her stall in order to block out some of the cold. Well, she fell in love with it at once, and for years she rubbed against it, hid behind it, peeked out from behind, over, and under it, and truly loved that awful, tattered thing.

Again, love played a part in making Daisy happy.

Daisy's tarp was her security blanket and made her feel safe.

Chapter 3

The next morning, when I was holding her milk for her, she nudged my thumb, took it into her mouth, and began to suck it. She would suck it, take a few more sips of milk, then suck some more, looking at me intently as if to say I was a funny-looking giraffe, but she loved me. Thumb-sucking became an important part of her daily routine. It made her feel so safe and good.

Rutherfurd told us giraffe like carrots, and boy, was he right! Daisy gobbled them up. At first we stuck them on the needlelike thorns of the thorn tree branches, then she took them right from our hand, and then—because we would bite off a piece from the whole carrot small enough for her to swallow—she couldn't wait for us to transfer them to our hand, so she began taking them right from our mouth. She was so gentle and, like a cow, had only bottom teeth at the front, so she never hurt us. But when other people saw us doing that, they would say, "Ugh, isn't that unsanitary?"

And we would always answer, "Yes, there's no telling what she might catch from us!" Giraffe mouths are

much cleaner than ours because giraffe don't eat meat and other things that decay. And Daisy's breath smelled wonderful, too, much better than human breath. Maybe some people have such sweet-smelling breath, but then I don't kiss too many people who eat only leaves.

Many friends came to see her, and everyone loved her. She was consumed by curiosity—about the cars coming and going, and about the children squealing with delight when they saw her. Although she liked the people, and enjoyed getting extra carrots, she distinguished Jock and me from the masses. She would not accept milk from anyone else, nor suck anyone else's thumb, and she would run up to us and kiss us through the railings whenever we were within reach.

We loved her so much. She had enchanted our lives —ah, but what about *her* life? It wasn't fair to her to be penned up; she should be free—so, six weeks later, we decided it was time to release her. What would she do when we opened the door? Would she trample us to get free and run away, never to be seen again? Would I never touch her or kiss her again? I was so afraid of losing her. Apprehensively we opened the gate and stood back and sang "Born Free."

She would not come out.

"Come on out, Daisy," we called, over and over, but she wouldn't move. Finally Jock lured her out with carrots. Standing right next to him, she looked around, cautiously took one step with him, stopped, looked around again, then took another step with him. He walked to a tree, pointed to the succulent branches, and said, "Taste those thorn leaves, Daisy." She did and loved them. But when Jock took a few steps away from her, she abandoned her favorite food and followed him.

The rest of the morning, the three of us walked around the lawn, while Daisy, like a child at a birthday party, tasted everything—the red flowers, the blue ones, the white gardenias, even the cactus. Never having seen a warthog before, she studied them in amazement. Then she spotted our horses, which were standing nearby looking at her in a state of shock. She started toward all of them to make friends, but, terrified, they ran off. "They'll get used to her," Jock said.

Daisy became very comfortable with the warthogs that live at Giraffe Manor.

Lunchtime came, and Jock and I walked up the steps to go into our house. As I was saying, "She won't come up the steps," she followed nonchalantly, as if giraffe go up and down steps every day. She was on her way into the house with us. If we hadn't pushed her head out of the front door, she would have walked right in. We peeped out the window at her. She looked so pitiful, we brought our lunch outside, sat on the steps, and ate it there. Seeing this, she folded herself onto the lawn and sat with us.

The rest of the day, she stayed just as close to us and continued to be interested in everything. By five o'clock, however, she was exhausted and went happily into her boma, drank her bottle, lay down in her soft bed of hay behind her tarp, and fell sound asleep.

The next days were carbon copies of the first. Always curious, she investigated everything. Then one day, Tom, Dick, and Harry came onto the lawn to see her. Giraffe are enormous—most people don't realize how gigantic they are. Eighteen feet is really tall, and three thousand pounds is really heavy. If Jock, who was six feet three, had walked underneath them, his head would not have touched the bottom of their stomachs. Up close, they seemed like gigantic dinosaurs.

We worried that the sight of giraffe again in her life might make her go off with them. Eighteen-foot Tom sauntered up to her and stood towering over nine-foot Daisy. She looked so tiny. Then, very slowly, the gentle giant lowered his head, sniffed her, and nuzzled her. Then he turned away and started to move off with the others. Daisy now had a choice: to move off into the forest with the old bulls or stay with us. The bulls stopped and turned around to Daisy as if to say, "Are you coming?" She looked at them for a few seconds, then ran up to Jock and hid behind him, as any child does with its mother in a scary new encounter. It was clear her choice was Jock—she had imprinted on him totally.

When Jock had to go back to work, Daisy was miserable. She just stood in one place all day long as if she were planted and growing there. Not even carrots would entice her to move; nor did she have any interest when the horses gradually approached her. But when she saw Jock's car coming back into the driveway, she'd run up to it, put her head in, give Jock a kiss, then run gleefully around in circles.

"It's so sad," I told Jock. "She loves you so much and is so unhappy when you're gone. But I have an idea. . . ."

"What's that?" he asked.

"Let's get another baby giraffe to keep her company."

Chapter 4

So it was back to the ranch, and the same movie starring Rutherfurd all over again. But this time it was a boy, and I fell in love again.

Perhaps because he was only three weeks old and therefore much smaller than Daisy, who was about three months when we captured her, we just picked him up like a great Dane and put him in the bus. He drank milk and let me touch him right away—he seemed delighted at being caught. As the butterflies on Daisy's back distinguished her, his markings were hearts. He had a perfect one on his cheek and another on his shoulder. He looked like a valentine. We named him Marlon and took him home.

We couldn't wait for poor little lonely Daisy, for whom we had gotten this friend to be with, to see him.

Stiff from his ride, he wobbled into the boma and was overjoyed to see her. She walked up to him and kicked him. Hard. He tried to nuzzle her, but she kicked him even harder. She hated him. We were afraid she would hurt him, so we separated them by putting up a slatted fence. We wanted her still to be able to see and touch him, hoping she would come to love him.

Marlon has the longest eyelashes!

He tried so hard to be near her all the time, and all she did, now that she couldn't kick him, was ignore him. Knowing he had to have someone to love and to love him back, and since Daisy was being so rotten, I took a little chair to the boma and sat with him all day, every day. I hung up a pretty curtain for him. He loved his bottle and being stroked and kissed (he had lipstick on his face most

Daisy and Marlon were separated but could still see and smell each other.

of the time!) and being told how much I loved him. After a week of my concentrating my love on Marlon and his concentrating his love on Daisy, he must have said, "Oh, forget Daisy. I'll pick the ugly one—at least she loves me." So Marlon imprinted on me.

Gentle Marlon loved his special blanket, too.

He also loved me because he thought I was a carrot machine. All he had to do was put his lips next to mine, and I ejected carrots into his mouth. When he was sure I was empty, he looked into my pockets to see if there were any more.

Having transferred his love to me, he became overly affectionate—sucking my thumb for long periods of time, rubbing his face against mine, chewing my hair and my buttons. He always wanted to be with me and touching me. Pretty soon we were even eating leaves together—well, I pretended to—because he didn't like eating alone.

Since Marlon had someone who loved him, he was very happy. But Daisy wasn't. The day we released Marlon, he was just standing there on the lawn minding his own business. All of a sudden, Daisy looked at him with a beady eye and charged the luckless little fellow, crashing into him with such a thud it nearly knocked him off his feet. Poor little Marlon—he was so sweet and gentle and had done nothing to attract her anger.

Jock and I were shocked at Daisy's violence. We finally concluded that she was jealous of Marlon. She had had undivided attention for several months and had grown used to being an only child. Now, although Jock still gave her her milk and I went up to her a few times a day with carrots, we had been concentrating almost solely on Marlon.

What should we do about this? Send Marlon to the animal orphanage? Or was she like all children everywhere who are jealous of new babies at first? We decided to try just leaving them alone, to see if she would get used to him.

But the next day, Daisy got sick. She just sat in her boma all day and wouldn't drink her milk or eat her grain or leaves or carrots. She wouldn't even suck Jock's thumb. She had a high temperature. We had six different vets, but none of them knew what was wrong with her. They had never had a giraffe patient before and didn't know what medicine to give. Jock and I sat with her and talked softly to her for three days, trying to give her some milk. She just sat there behind her tarp and looked at us with sad, sick eyes and would not eat or drink. We were so worried.

Then our friend who had told us how important love is said we were probably overfeeding her, so we didn't try to force her anymore. Sure enough, in a few days, whether it was because she had eaten too much or because she was now certain we loved her, she got better.

Daisy needed to know we loved her.

But by now Marlon was jealous. One day he somehow managed to get the little folding chair I sat on in his boma around his neck. He ran around with it on as if he were carrying a schoolbag. Then he got lots of attention while we tried for hours to get it off.

We let them both out together again, and for the next few weeks Daisy ignored him, but she didn't kick him anymore.

Marlon and his folding chair.

The horses began to steal the hay from Daisy's boma and eat it. So one night Daisy followed Marlon into his boma so she could rest on soft hay instead of the hard ground. When she sat down next to him, he was so pleased he made funny faces for her, then he nuzzled her. She looked at him a minute and then nuzzled him back! So at last they were friends. And from then on, they were always together—playing, sleeping, eating.

Daisy and Marlon could tell time. At exactly six, every evening, they went back into their boma, drooling for their supper. After we'd fed them and stroked them and talked to them, and they'd sucked our thumbs, they'd lie down and sleep, even though the door was always open. They felt so safe and happy there.

After a while the horses lost their fear and came up while we fed Daisy and Marlon their grain. Cautiously they began to put their heads into the pans. Daisy and Marlon seemed glad to share their food with them, and soon the horses were their friends, too.

Daisy and Marlon never left our property, but they ate almost all of it. Everyone else has trees and shrubs that grow, but ours got smaller every day. Soon the gardenias and nasturtiums and bougainvillea disappeared all together. What we had to do then was offer them a flower or shrub before we planted it, and what they *didn't* eat we planted. "If only they had something else to do except destroy our garden . . ." I told Jock. To entertain them, I bought a big beach ball, which they kicked around the lawn, *then* destroyed our garden.

Finally, Daisy came over to Marlon and nuzzled him!

One day Jock brought home an enormous blow-up giraffe to see if they would play with it. But they merely walked up to it, sniffed it, and walked over and nuzzled us. They weren't dummies—they knew a real giraffe from a toy one.

They loved us, and we loved them so much, too. They brought so much joy into our lives. We became concerned about the rest of the giraffe left back on our friend's ranch.

"You can't bring them all here, Betty," Jock told me nervously.

"No, but we can move them to the safety of a game park."

So we got a giraffe-sitter, sadly bid Daisy and Marlon good-bye for a few months, and went to the United States to try to raise money to move the remaining Rothschild giraffe to safety.

Chapter 5

We established the African Fund for Endangered Wildlife (AFEW) in 1978. We had a "Save a Wild Child" program, where anyone who donated $500 (what it cost to move a giraffe to safety) could name it himself. This is why the Rothschild giraffe have such funny names: a Catholic lady named one "John Paul" after the Pope; we also have "Pan Am," "the Mets," "Intercontinental Hotel," and lots of names like "Aunt Mary."

We had Giraffe Galas in many cities and raised enough money to translocate the first twenty-three of these endangered animals to the safety of a game park.

Remember I mentioned the African in the gas station who never saw a giraffe before? Well, 80 percent of Africans have never seen the game. They are too poor to have cars, the only way one is allowed into a game park. Game parks are expensive—only the tourists can afford them. But tourists from all over the world bring a lot of money to the country and provide thousands of Africans with jobs. Without the animals, tourists would not come to Africa, and without tourists, the Africans would not have jobs. So we must save the game, first so that the

This giraffe is being moved to safety from poachers, thanks to many donations.

people will survive, and second so that the beautiful animals will live. Jock and I wondered how we could teach the Africans this.

We had an idea, for which we got a grant from a U.S. foundation, and acquired the primeval forest next to our property. There we built the first educational nature center in independent Africa. Every day now we bus African schoolchildren out to the center. Many of them, the poorest of the poor, have never seen an animal or walked in a forest. You can imagine their delight when they not only see but touch and feed Daisy and Marlon for the first time! Then they walk through the primeval forest and learn about saving the trees and land. Afterward, at

African children by the thousands come to our center to meet Daisy and Marlon.

the center, we give them milk and cookies and show them a film about conservation. We bring two thousand children each month to teach them they must preserve these animals.

Poachers kill zebra to sell their skins for rugs, poach elephant to sell their ivory tusks, and kill giraffe just for the hair from their tails to make bracelets.

Wouldn't it be terrible if Daisy and Marlon were killed to become bracelets?

And wouldn't it be terrible if all the giraffe were poached and our grandchildren would have to ask, "What was a giraffe?"

But with the help of people who care, perhaps we can still save the few wild animals left in the world.

Would you like to help?

If so, send your tax-deductible contribution
to
The African Fund for Endangered Wildlife (AFEW)
1512 Bolton Street
Baltimore, Maryland 21217
or

If you would like to come on safari, write to us for additional information. You can stay at the Giraffe Manor, as the Leslie-Melville house is now called, and all proceeds from your stay go to help save endangered species.

(Daisy, who has babies of her own now, will put her head in your second-floor bedroom window and thank you.)

Index

About the Author

Betty Leslie-Melville was born and raised in Baltimore, Maryland. Her love affair with the Rothschild giraffe began with Daisy and developed into a larger drive, now credited with saving the entire Rothschild subspecies. Together with her late husband, Jock, Betty founded the African Fund for Endangered Wildlife, Inc. (AFEW), a conservation group now involved with saving the endangered black rhinoceros, as well, from extinction. She and her husband collectively wrote five books about their extraordinary lives in Kenya. This is Betty's second solo work. Betty Leslie-Melville divides her time between Giraffe Manor in Nairobi, Kenya, where seven Rothschild giraffe roam free across the lawns, and New York City.